MW01170167

My Journey to Catholicism

Sheldon Cohen

ACTA
ASSISTING CHRISTIANS TO ACT
PUBLICATIONS

To My Wonderful Wife, Leona

My Journey to Catholicism
by Sheldon Cohen

Edited by Gregory F. Augustine Pierce
Cover Design by Tom A. Wright
Typesetting by Garrison Publications

Copyright © 1996 by Sheldon Cohen

Published by ACTA Publications
              Assisting Christians To Act
              4848 N. Clark Street
              Chicago, IL 60640
              800-397-2282

Library of Congress Catalog number: 96-084020

ISBN: 0-87946-139-X

Printed in the United States of America

00 99 98 97 96 5 4 3 2 1 First Printing

I.

"Shelly, you don't have to convert to Catholicism," my neighbor Suzie said. "You can stay on the fence and not make a decision. That way no one will get hurt and you can keep your options open. You might change your mind."

I remember when Suzie said those words in 1970. My family lived in New Jersey then, in a lovely community with good schools, many friends, and a bright future on the horizon. Looking back, from my vantage point in California 25 years later, it seems like a lifetime ago. But before those events disappear from view, I feel compelled to put them down in some intelligible chronicle. Perhaps reliving those times will help me with my faith now, and perhaps my story in some small way might help others.

Shelly and Mom

II.

I was born of Jewish parents in Brooklyn, New York, during the great depression. We lived in a cold-water apartment in a neighborhood that had a mixture of many ethnic groups. There were Italians, Irish, Germans and a smattering of others. Religiously, the neighborhood was predominantly Catholic with a small minority of Jews. Religion wasn't important to me then, but what was important was whether I could play stick-ball or not. Don't get me wrong, life wasn't that rosy. There were many moments of religious bigotry where fists flew and angry words were said. But mainly, we got along. We had to. We were all in the same economic boat—poor.

My schooling was not very unusual. In those days, the public schools were terrific. There was no busing, just a short walk down the street to P.S. 122 and four blocks further to Eastern District High School. Brooklyn College was just a short bus ride to Flatbush, a more affluent section of the borough.

If I were to say I liked school I'd be fibbing. I liked baseball, roller skating, and general street mayhem. That is, until I discovered the world of music.

It happened this way. My brother had studied the violin and now it was my turn. Mom took me by the hand and brought me to the local violin teacher, Lydia Coval. "Here he is, Lydia . . . he's all yours . . . . one dollar a lesson . . . that will be fine," Mom said.

Fine for you, Mom, but not for me. Lydia scared the daylights out of me. She wasn't a pretty woman and hardly ever smiled, and, besides, I really wanted to be outside on the street with the guys.

I took two lessons and quit. Mom was distraught. Lydia probably thought it was for the best. I was elated. Now I could get back to serious things like hanging out with my friends. Music took a backseat to ball playing and other activities that are better left unsaid here.

High school now loomed on the horizon and with the usual trepidation about school, my buddies—girls included—entered the hallowed halls of Eastern District High School. Studies were serious business, but playing ball still occupied a lot of my time. I had the grades to prove it: No straight "A's" for me.

It was in high school that it happened. The moment when it all came together, when I became a willful slave to music. It was a moment I will cherish for the rest of my life.

His name was Mr. Freundlich. A tall, lanky, balding man with a mild disposition and a twinkle in his eye. He was the music teacher and band director. I met him early in my high school career and, fortunately for me, listened to what he had to say. He was the one who opened the door, the catalyst. He was, in retrospect, my first mentor. To him I owe a great debt of gratitude.

The music program in high school afforded students a chance to learn how to play instruments. I volunteered to study the clarinet and Mr. Freundlich taught me. Not only me, but my longtime friend, Harvey, as well. We both attacked the silver plated clarinets with a vengeance. Perhaps, "playing" is the wrong word . . . "honking" might be more appropriate. In any event, there I was in a band, playing music I liked, music that made my emotions do hand-stands. I was now part of something new . . . something beautiful . . . something that seemed to consume all my thoughts. It was, to put it mildly, "thrilling."

Not only did I avidly pursue the clarinet, but now I returned to "dear" Lydia and began to study the violin. No more did she appear as an unsmiling, forbidding lady. Now she became the storehouse of musical knowledge—knowledge that I sorely wanted. The days weren't long enough. Music had captured my soul. It became my entire focus, my constant preoccupation, and I devoured it with a passion.

Of course, there were always girls. As a pimply teenager, I pursued them with vigor and enjoyed many moments of high passion. Please understand, in those days "high passion" was holding hands and maybe a kiss in a hallway. But still, it was a very exciting pastime. I was 16 when I met the person with whom I would spend the rest of my life. Her name was Leona Levy, a nice Jewish girl from the same neighborhood, with the same economic background.

We dated a few times and met occasionally at parties and at school. She was a shy, beautiful, dark-haired girl with bangs. . . . oh, how I loved those bangs! (As well as loving the rest of her too.) I surely noticed her slim figure and dark eyes. On top of it all, she could really roller skate! Roller skating was big then. We would go to the local roller-rink and spend the afternoon holding hands during the pair skating and talk until we were hoarse.

III.

My religious thinking at the time was slim to none. My family always attended High Holy Day services (Yom Kippur and Rosh Hashonah) in temple. We kept a kosher home, but that was the extent of our religion. We never read from the Bible or discussed religious questions. That was left for others to do. For my family, the focus was, "Will we be able to pay the bills this month and how might we improve our family situation?"

My grandparents lived in the same brownstone house as we, but in a separate apartment. They spoke very little English, yet somehow I was able to communicate with them without having to resort to Yiddish. That would have been extremely difficult. Although I understand spoken Yiddish, I am incapable of putting together an intelligible sentence. However, we did communicate—mainly about food. Grandma was a terrific cook and there was always something to eat on her wood-burning stove. I can almost taste those delicious potato pancakes now.

My extended family consisted of many aunts, uncles and cousins, who lived as modestly as we. They lived in other parts of the city. Periodically, we would visit them and usually had a good time, except when mother had "words" with someone. Then we would hastily exit the house and trudge off to the subway with Mom bending Dad's ear. If they didn't want me to understand what they were saying, they would speak in Yiddish. I don't think they realized that I knew enough to understand them. In any event, I was too busy reading comic books to care.

Sunday mornings were difficult for me. I'd sit on my front stoop, baseball glove in hand, waiting for my friends to come home from Transfiguration Church. Finally, they'd round the corner dressed in their best ties and jackets. I could hardly wait for them to change clothes so we could get our baseball game started. There was no time to lose. Monday was a school day.

Like every good Jewish boy, I attended Hebrew school and had my Bar-Mitzvah. I did not like Hebrew studies and for that matter did not like the rabbi. But going to Hebrew school was something that had to be done, something that had to be endured. I completed the course of study, and to this day I still shudder at the memory of that experience. I guess religion didn't have a place in my life then, but what I did learn was that my Jewish heritage was to be appreciated. Being Jewish gave me a real sense of pride. After all, 4,000 years of history is a long time.

Perhaps if I had been born in another place and in another time, the Jewish religion would have meant more to me. But, in America, in the first part of the 20th century, we Jews had been given an opportunity to shed our fears of oppression and were allowed to pursue the Great American dream along with everyone else. Hard work and perseverance alone would pay off. I felt that whatever I wanted to accomplish with my life could be done without reliance on my Jewish heritage. Religious belief or practice would not be a factor in my achieving personal success.

Shelly at Camp Chaffee, Arkansas

IV.

Because my brother was serving in the army during World War II, his welfare became the main preoccupation of the Cohen household. As I recall, my mother and sister spent many hours writing letters and sending food packages to him in Europe. As for myself, I was much too busy collecting pictures of naval battles and building model airplanes. I'm sure it was a stressful time for my family and caused them many a sleepless night.

My involvement in world events came a little later, during the Korean War, when I decided to enlist in the army. Mother and Dad were not happy with my decision and were only reluctantly supportive. Artillery training at Camp Chaffee, Arkansas, was an experience I would not exchange for anything. In spite of the rigors of Army basic training, I found myself being placed in leadership roles I had not experienced before. Each day brought me new and exciting challenges that, in retrospect, changed my whole life. No more was I that gangling teenager, no more that unsure Shelly. Now emerging was a thinking, motivated, and idealistic man. The army was good for me and laid a very strong foundation for many of my future endeavors.

During my tour of duty in the army, I found some time to reflect on religious matters. Services for Jewish soldiers were held every Friday night and I attended regularly. Those services were vastly different from the ones I had experienced as a child. First of all, the prayers were said mostly in English and I could understand their meaning. Secondly, the people in attendance were for the most part my own age. I related to them and enjoyed the overall experience, although I still didn't have a deep appreciation of the tenets of my faith. That would come much later.

It was during a short furlough, before going overseas, that I became reacquainted with Leona. It was a Thursday. I was home on leave and much to my chagrin found myself without a date for a Friday night outing with friends. What to do? Well, there was always my little black book. And there was her name, Leona Levy. (Before I had left for the Army, I promised I would write to her, but I had failed to do so. Maybe if I told a little white lie all would be okay. So, I called her and lied. It worked, and I've never regretted that one ethical lapse.) Leona went out with me on Friday, Saturday, Sunday, and every day for the rest of my leave. I had found that special someone. Before I went overseas she promised to wait for my return. Then we would be married.

After serving for a year in Europe, I returned home, married Leona, and spent the next seven years going to school at night and working during the day in the mailroom at the National Broadcasting Company. It was there my future in music really began. I interviewed for a job in the music department and got it. This was surely the hand of God working in my life. My love of music

14

would be fulfilled in ways I could never have imagined. I learned my craft from the best in the music industry and it has held me in good stead all these many years.

Shelly and Leona

V.

As in every life's journey, there are highs and lows. One of my lows came when I lost my job at NBC. In 1960 we had just moved to a small house in a suburban community in New Jersey when the axe fell. We had very little money in the bank, so I immediately began calling everyone in my address book to try to find work. Eventually, I did find jobs as a freelance composer, arranger and all round music person. Again, in retrospect it seemed that God was watching over me when I needed Him most.

Life in the suburbs was a real growing experience for me and for my family. Would you believe there were trees and grass there? Something that was rare in the concrete jungles of Brooklyn. We became acclimated to our new surroundings and quickly began living that great American dream—a house, a job, and a lawn that needed mowing every Saturday morning. Our neighbors were mostly expatriates from the city, so we had much in common. They represented the same ethnic cross-section of people we had experienced growing up. The Irish, the Italians and many other ethic groups had found their way upwards and outwards to the wilds of northern New Jersey.

New Jersey wasn't quite the same as Brooklyn. Here in the suburbs, it seemed, we had more time to enjoy our surroundings. There were hikes in the woods and trips to the duck pond. We had white snow in winter and an abundance of flowers in the spring, and there was lots of community involvement in school and in places of worship. It surely was a very different life style.

After a few months in our new home, we were visited by two people who were members of the local reformed temple, Temple Beth Or. They came to our house to ask if we would like to join their small but growing community. There was no building yet, but the local firehouse was rented on Friday nights so that we might be able to have services. Leona and I spoke with them and decided that—not necessarily for our personal religious growth but for the benefit of our children—it would be necessary to become members of a temple.

So we joined Temple Beth Or and became involved in many of its activities. We found comfort with people of our own faith. Looking back at those early days, I find myself smiling with pride that I was somewhat instrumental in establishing a Temple in that area, as well as making many wonderful friends along the way.

However, there was a part of my Jewish heritage that eluded me. I had very little knowledge of the essence of my faith. To me the temple seemed more of a social organization than a spiritual one. Apparently the time was not yet right for me to gain a deeper understanding of the spiritual . God's time and my time were not the same.

VI.

If I wasn't growing spiritually, I certainly was expanding my professional career. Composing songs, writing jingles for commercials, making arrangements for recordings and even creating the music for an off-Broadway musical were the avenues I was successfully pursuing. On the home front, we had expanded as well. Three wonderful boys—Steven, Howard, and Robert—were now part of the "Jersey Cohens." We were all thriving in our little Cape Cod home. (Well, maybe it was getting a wee-bit crowded!)

One day in 1967, Leona and I were out driving in a not-too-distant community called Woodcliff Lake. Yes, there was a small body of water there, but that's not the only thing we saw. We also saw apple orchards and a new development being built on its fringe. We stopped, took one look, then packed our bags. Once again, we were off on a new adventure.

The community which we now called home was something very special. Our house was large and comfortable with lots of room on the outside for three athletic boys to roam. The neighbors were mostly our own age and had gobs of children. Everyone got along just fine. There were no fences and for the most part no petty animosities. Our attitude and that of our neighbors was "Let's raise our kids in as wholesome an atmosphere as we possibly can." And we did. There were the ever-popular stick-ball games (adults vs. kids), sledding in winter, block parties and even movies under the stars. Once we closed the street and invited the mayor to come and judge a "Decorate-Your-Lawnmower" contest. The Cohens lost.

At this point in my musical career, I became associated with *The Tonight Show with Johnny Carson.* I became the assistant music conductor and on occasion I even got to conduct the orchestra. Johnny would fondly refer to me during his monologue as "The Kosher Montavani." Spiritually, though, I was on hold. I had been elected second vice president at Temple Beth Or, but that elusive understanding of God and my relationship with Him was not yet at hand. Yes, I sat through Friday night services and understood the prayers, but I never felt the elation of really knowing God. He, for the time being, was on a shelf somewhere.

VII.

Have you ever looked back in your life and remembered an event that somehow stood out boldly from all the rest? An event that brought about a profound change in your thinking and in your whole approach to life? The following series of events in my life were of that kind. Some, indeed were sad and some happy, but all propelled me to a more meaningful existence. Those milestones surely helped to define who I am today. They were the bricks and mortar on which my life would be built. Again, I believe it was God's fine hand at work, only I didn't realize it at the time.

It all started in a rather innocuous way when Leona and I decided to finish our basement. All that we needed was some expertise in woodworking and construction. Unfortunately, those skills were in short supply with me. So, I consulted with two of my neighbors, Tony Prisco and Mike Jordan. They were the ones who could help me. We conferred about the project and then they gave me a list of supplies we would need. The enterprise soon took on monumental proportions, with everyone getting into the act. The women made the coffee while the men worked into the wee hours of the morning. We laughed, we drank, and I banged my finger with a hammer. Tony and Mike completed the job in record time, while all along the way the women applauded our efforts. Of course, Leona and I offered to pay for the work, but there were no takers. So we did the next best thing and took all of them out for a superb lobster dinner at a local restaurant. A wonderful time was had by all. The evening was still young when we finished dinner, so we continued the festivities at our home. Around midnight, the discussion turned to religion. We each took a turn sharing our personal belief or non-belief in the deity.

I think it's an important rule that there are two subjects not to be discussed if friendships are to last: politics and religion. I'm afraid we broke the rule on that occasion. A heated discussion ensued and I found myself espousing the position of being unsure whether there was a God or not—pure agnosticism. Others spoke of Christ, the Son of God, of God the Father, and of the Holy Spirit. Indeed, this part of the conversation was totally foreign to me. Around 1:00 A.M. the party broke up. We said our goodbyes and thanked everyone again for our new basement. Mike and True Jordan were the last ones to leave. Then True said these memorable words: "Would you mind if I came over tomorrow morning and spoke with you about God?"

"Sure," we said. "Come on over. We'll have some coffee and continue where we left off." Little did we know that such an innocent invitation for coffee would have so profound an effect on our lives.

VII.

True is a woman whose Catholic faith runs deep. She has a quiet way about her that is not found in many people. Her voice is soft and fits well with her demeanor. She is always eager to please and never overbearing, but it is her unshakable belief in God that comes through. Everything she does says, "This is for the greater glory of God." Whether it be a menial task or one of a transcendent spiritual nature, it is always done in His name. I guess God had touched True in some special way when she asked if she might speak with us about Him. I've often wondered what was going through her mind at the time. Perhaps, she saw a need in our lives and felt she might be instrumental in filling that need.

As she said she would, True arrived early the next day. We had coffee and spoke about God. I don't remember the exact content of our first discussion, but I do remember it didn't end there. Those morning meetings went on for almost a year. At least three times a week, True would come to us or we would visit with her for breakfast and discussion. Initially, our conversation was about my Jewish God, the one whose existence I doubted. I asked a thousand questions and she an-

swered every one of them. When she lacked the knowledge to respond, she postponed her answer until her
next visit. If she couldn't find the answer herself, she
would call someone at her church for help. In any event,
there was always an answer to my questions, albeit not
always a satisfying one.

At times our conversations became heated and
caused all of us to feel some sense of frustration. But we
persevered and I believe everyone got something out of
those meetings. About three months into our morning
get-togethers, I felt the need to pursue the question of
God's existence with the people at my temple. I spoke
with many of my Jewish friends about their beliefs, and
to my surprise I found they had similar questions in their
minds, although most of them didn't appear to have an
urgent need for answers. I even had conversations with
our rabbi. Unfortunately, he didn't have satisfactory
answers for me either.

Yet something in me kept driving me to find out
more about the God who was so important in my
neighbor True's life.

VIII.

Our very first visit to a Catholic church came in December. True and Mike invited our family to attend a Christmas Mass. We accepted and brought our boys with us. We sat with the Jordan's and their three girls, and as we sat there, they explained the various parts of the Mass. I noticed there were very definite similarities to our own Jewish services, but the part of the Mass that effected me most was when the people returned from receiving communion. Their demeanor seemed to be one of peace and serenity. I had never witnessed such a phenomena before. What was in that small wafer that seemed to transform those people? Had God really become one with them? It was a very difficult concept for me to grasp.

There is a word in the English language that I hardly ever use. That word is "surrender." Now it was time for me to not only use that word, but to do it. I had finally come to believe that God exists and that it is He who is responsible for all I see around me—the earth, the heavens and my fellow human beings. I surrendered, and I found that I felt more Jewish than I had ever felt before. After all, it was we Jews, starting with Abraham who had accepted the one God as the only God. It was the God/human relationship that had set the moral tone for Judeo/Christian behavior for the last 4,000 years.

I was at a plateau, a level of acceptance in my mind that was very satisfying. Yet deep down I knew there was more, and apparently so did True. For her next step was to ask us, "Would you mind if I spoke with you about Jesus?" Now thing's were really getting out of hand! I had come a long way to finally believe in my Jewish God, only to be faced with yet another question: Is there validity in the Christian belief that Jesus is the Son of that same God? My response to True was simple. "Sure, we can talk about Jesus, but I'll tell you right now, you are *not* going to convince me. My mind is made up. I've found the God I believe in, and that's that. There's no more for me. I'm satisfied."

The next day, True came once again for coffee and we were off. More questions. More answers. And more frustrations. Leona and I sat through those sessions, then spoke privately about our beliefs and disbeliefs. We were both on the same track, but our timetables were different. Unbeknownst to me, Leona was beginning to accept Jesus as the fulfillment of God's promise. I, on the other hand, was not. I could not. It seemed like a negation of my Jewish heritage. After all, look how much the Jews have suffered in the name of Christianity. How could I ever accept Jesus? Yet we continued to explore many of the tenets of Catholicism and had some long and sometimes tearful arguments with True. I challenged. She parried. I got angry. She became peaceful. I sulked. She consoled. I guess we ran the full gamut of human emotions. But as in the poem, "The Hounds of Heaven," True kept on pursuing me.

IX.

In the spring of 1971, a series of events occurred that helped to dispel my dark clouds of uncertainty. I had been asked to write a musical piece for my oldest son Steven's high school band, and to that end chose a narrative musical format. The subject would be "Peace and Love." My problem with the topic was finding a believable text. What could I say to the children of the 70's about peace and love? It was a large problem.

I mentioned the project to True and she suggested I speak with a young priest at her church, Father Ken St. Amand. "He might be able to give you some direction," she said. I accepted her suggestion, called Fr. Ken, and invited him to the house for lunch. He showed up as planned, had lunch, and then joined me at the piano where I played my piece for him. He helped a great deal in getting me on the right track, but it was his final statement that really did me in. He said, "Would you mind if I prayed for you, Shelly?" No one had ever asked for permission to pray for me. We prayed as a group in Temple and prayed for others and perhaps for ourselves collectively, but no one had ever said "Shelly, may I pray for you." I guess I said "Yes" because the next few minutes were meant solely for me. Fr. Ken prayed that God would help me, not only for guidance with the composition I was writing but also with clearing my mind so I might be able to accept the fullness of the Lord's gifts. It's hard for me to describe the feeling I had at that moment. Here was another human being asking God to intercede in my life. That was pretty "heavy stuff." I was quite moved by the moment and thought about it for a long while.

The next incident happened several weeks later. It seems Steven had gotten involved with a teenage musical group sponsored by Fr. Ken's church. They were in need of some advice and asked me for some profes-sional guidance. I invited them (about 10 youngsters) to the house for sandwiches and a sharing of their musical problems. We gathered on the back porch and away we went. After about an hour of eating and talking, the conversation drifted to religious subjects. A lively rap session followed with many points of view being espoused. I, for the most part, listened. Then a curious thing happened. There was a moment of silence and then someone said, "Let's pray for Mr. Cohen." I was dumbstruck. It took me a while to recover and grasp what was happening. Here were 10 young people—my own Jewish son among them—praying for me. It was a new and very unusual experience. I know I shed a tear and realize it affected me in a very deep and positive way.

Our Lady of Mercy Church, the church to which the Jordans belonged, was sponsoring a charismatic re-newal group and they invited us to attend a few of their meetings. Here was something very different for me and my family. Total strangers had extended their hands in friendship to us with no questions asked. It didn't seem to matter that we were Jewish. All that mattered was that we were interested and so were welcomed.

Leona and I sat and listened while the people prayed. They all seemed to accept God's presence in their lives. There were no doubts, no reservations, just total assurance that He existed and that He was always there for them. Strange as it may seem, I found myself wanting to share my Jewish heritage with them. It came in the form of reading from my Hebrew prayer book, then translating the prayers into English. They seemed to get a big charge out of that. In retrospect, it may have been a little presumptuous of me, but it seemed the right thing to do at the time. In any event, the group didn't mind. On the contrary, they were quite taken with the whole thing.

Mike and True Jordan and Children

X.

The next sequence of events is a little blurry in my mind. I began to study my Judaic background with much more vigor than I had ever done in the past and continued to speak with my Jewish friends about who this God of ours was. Leona, as I later found out, had quietly accepted Jesus but was reluctant to reveal her decision, fearing she might unduly influence me. True continued her visits and I continued my resistance. There was still much more for me to learn about the Son of God.

It was in August of 1971 when the whole situation became resolved. True and Mike were away on vacation and Leona and I were having our usual conversation about religious matters. We had reached a stone wall, or at least I had. At this point Leona suggested we call the rectory at Our Lady of Mercy Church and ask Fr. Ken if he had a few minutes to speak with us. When we arrived he was in his office. He was waiting for a group of people who were coming to church for an afternoon prayer session. We spoke for a while about God, Jesus and the Church. Leona and I asked several questions and spent a pleasant half hour with him. Soon, the people began to arrive for their prayer meeting, so Leona and I rose to leave. Fr. Ken asked if we would like to stay. We said yes.

First the people shared some of their experiences of the past week and then they began to pray. I listened for a few moments, but I couldn't stay. My mind was not tuned into what they were doing. I was preoccupied with other thoughts and quietly left the room. Fr. Ken followed and, sensing my discomfort, asked if he might be of some help. I said, "No, this is my problem and I'll have to work it out in my own way."

On a table in the room outside was a Bible. As Fr. Ken stood silently by, I reached for it and randomly flipped through its pages. As I recall, I stopped at a paragraph from Hebrews. It read something like this: "Do not fear what others will say about your love of Jesus." At that moment, the thoughts that flooded my mind were many and confused. Was this the root of my problem? Was I fearful of what my family and friends would say if I believed in Jesus? Would it destroy all the things I held so dear?

Then a new thought began to emerge. If I had lived at the time of Jesus, and had witnessed His miracles and heard Him speak, would I have followed His teaching no matter what the consequences? The answer was suddenly there. *Yes, I would have followed Him. He would have been a tremendous influence in my life.* And so it ended. I had asked my last question. I had finally made a decision. I had taken a giant leap of "faith." No more vacillation. Now it was time for trust, acceptance and love. I began to cry.

Fr. Ken was the first to hear my words of acceptance. I looked up and said, "Fr. Ken, I have no more questions. I accept Jesus as my Savior." I'm sure Fr. Ken understood the depth of my decision and was moved by the event. We walked back into the other room where the prayer service was still in progress. I made my announcement. Leona, with tears in her eyes, kissed me. Then the others joined in and congratulated me on my decision. It was a joyous moment for all.

After a short time we drove home, or maybe I should say, "flew home." I don't quite remember the sequence of events but I do remember that True and Mike had just returned from their vacation. Can you imagine their reaction when I shared the good news with them? There were many tears and many hosannas. But most of all, there was lots and lots of love. What a very special moment for all of us.

Steven, Howard, Robert Cohen

XI.

We told Fr. Ken that we were ready to be baptized. He questioned us and felt that the year-long dialogue with True had been sufficient instruction. He said we would be received into the Church in a few days. Things moved quiet rapidly after that. Leona, our son Steven, and I decided we wanted to be baptized together in the faith. Steven had, without my knowledge, been actively studying the faith. Here we were, three people in the same family, deciding to follow the teachings of Jesus. Wow!

However, there was a problem—a very large problem. The difficulty was with our second son, Howard. He was scheduled for his Bar Mitzvah on the coming Friday, and a big celebration with family and friends was planned. It was an event we certainly had to consider. Our solution was this: Steven, Leona and I would be baptized on Monday night and would keep our secret from friends and family until after the Bar Mitzvah had taken place. That way, according to our thinking, no one would be hurt by our decision, and Howard would reap the benefit of the years of religious study he had just completed. Remember though, that the best laid plans of mice and men—you know! But I'm getting ahead of myself.

An announcement was made in church at Monday morning Mass. The Cohens were to be baptized that evening and anyone wishing to attend the ceremony would be welcome. We drove to the church that night and found 90 people waiting to witness our Baptism. I remember speaking to the congregation. I said something like, "This is not a hastily made decision but one prompted by long and arduous study. I offer myself as a follower of Christ. Whatever He wants of me I will do."

The ceremony was beautiful. All who were present laid hands on us. Then we were bathed in the cleansing waters of Baptism. When the water was poured on my head, I distinctly remember refusing to use a towel to wipe away the excess. I said, "Let it stay on my head for a little while longer, it feels wonderful." That special moment of Baptism still remains fresh in my mind and to this day has great meaning for me. It's a pity people born into the faith do not have a memory of their own Baptism. I believe it would serve them well to have a recollection of that special moment.

The rest of the week was spent getting ready for Howard's Bar Mitzvah. There was food to prepare, decorations to be hung, and visiting relatives to be picked up at the bus stop. I took Friday as a vacation day and stayed home to help Leona with the final preparations. At about three in the afternoon, I headed for the bus stop to bring home the first contingent of relatives. When I returned, Leona's face was ashen and her eyes were red from crying. I took her away from our guests and spoke with her. She had just received a phone call from our rabbi. He had found out about our Baptism, and as far as he was concerned the Bar Mitzvah would not take place. Now it was my turn to feel the pain.

We decided to call the pastor at Our Lady of Mercy Church and ask if there was anything he could do to help the situation. He quickly called the rabbi and a solution was found. Howard would have his Bar Mitzvah, but I would not be allowed to take part in the ceremony. That is, I would not be permitted to read from the Torah, nor would I be able to pass the Torah on to my son. Acting in my place would be my father-in-law. It was not a happy Cohen family who attended their son's Bar Mitzvah that Friday night. It was indeed one of the saddest moments in our lives. Every one of our temple friends were aware of the situation, and although they attended the service their faces reflected their disbelief and sadness. We fully understood their anguish and tried to put up a brave front, but it was without doubt one of the most difficult times in our lives. The only consolation we had was that all the while the people of Our Lady of Mercy Church were praying for us.

Fortunately, the next day I was scheduled to travel with my family to California for two weeks of taping *The Tonight Show*. It was a blessing in disguise, for it gave us a chance to regroup and prepare for the time when we would once again meet our friends from the temple. I remember writing several personal letters of explanation to my closest friends and upon our return from California had dinner with most of them. We explained our long and difficult journey and hoped they would understand. It took a while, but eventually most everyone came around.

Howard's Bar Mitzvah

XII.

We settled into Our Lady of Mercy Church and became regular parishioners. I was expecting to relax and enjoy my new position, but it seemed God had other plans in mind. Plans I could never in my wildest dreams have imagined.

About two weeks after returning from California, I received a phone call from a gentleman at the church. He knew about me and my family and also knew of my professional musical background. His purpose for calling was to ask if I might want to start a choir at the church. They were in need of someone with the expertise to pull it together. I explained to him that my knowledge of liturgical music was extremely limited. I was trained solely as a violinist and composer of jingles and popular music. In school, although exposed to choral music, it held no special interest for me.

It was then I remembered my promise at the Baptism, "Whatever He wants of me, I will do." Well, here was my first opportunity. Would I do it? I told the man on the phone I felt inadequate for the task, but I would give it my best shot.

That was all he had to hear. The next thing I knew I was sitting at my piano writing music for the Mass. Believe it or not, I couldn't put the notes down on the paper fast enough. In about a weeks time, I had completed The Gloria, The Sanctus, The Great Amen, and many of the other sung parts of the Mass. All that remained to be done was to enlist some singers and begin rehearsals.

The volunteers showed up on a Thursday. There were 50 of them, all sizes and shapes, young and old alike. Their reason for being there was just like mine—wanting to be of service to God and His Church. We started with a prayer and launched into the music.

My religious compositions had an unusual flavor to them. There was a hint of my Hebraic heritage and a contemporary beat—neither of which had ever been heard in Our Lady of Mercy Church before. The accompanying instruments were different as well. They were an odd collection at best. There was the traditional organ, a guitar, a harp, and my son Steven playing the conga drums. The sound was unique, but it seemed to fit my compositions. Needless to say, I had many reservations about how the congregation might react to this music. But that was quickly dispelled when we sang our first Mass.

From entrance hymn to exit hymn we sang with joy and love, and when it was over the applause was deafening. I acknowledged the congregation, then turned to the choir and asked if this was normal. They replied with an emphatic "No." This was a very unusual occurrence. Every Sunday after that the choir Mass was packed with people of all ages, and thunderous applause echoed through the church when the service was over. I asked myself if this was what God had in mind for me? Was I to bring a new kind of music to His Church? Was this going to be my mission?

Johnny Carson and Shelly

XIII.

    The Cohens stayed in New Jersey for another year before our next adventure began. But in that year, I learned much about liturgy and how important it is for the people.

    My family, although temporarily diverse in their religious beliefs, was also changing. Howard and Robert were now studying to become Catholics. Upon completion of their studies they joined with us as believers in Jesus. Now, we were whole. Now we were once again a unified family.

    In 1972 came the announcement. The Tonight Show was moving to California. Along with a few others—Ed McMahon, Doc Severinsen and Tommy Newson among them—I was asked if I wanted to go. There would be a job waiting for me. Leona and I discussed the proposition, then once again began packing. This time, though, the move was especially difficult. Not only would we be leaving our relatives in New York, but we would be separating from Our Lady of Mercy Church, the choir, and the many friends we had in New Jersey. It was a heart-rending decision but one we knew we had to make. The tears flowed freely when we said "goodbye" to True and Mike. They had been like brother and sister to us. For me personally, leaving the choir was extremely difficult. There was an undefinable bond that had grown between us. We prayed together and shared each others' joys and sorrows. It was truly an unusual choir-conductor relationship, and to this day I am still in touch with many of them.

Leona and I had been to Los Angeles on several occasions, but when you spend most of your time in a hotel, you don't really get to know a place. Now we were faced with finding a new home, good schools for the children, and a church where we might feel comfortable.

The house we found was located without too much difficulty (on Galilee Street) except that it was in the process of being built and wouldn't be ready for immediate occupancy. So the five of us checked into a motel not too far from the NBC studios.

But again, God reached out and touched us. A family living in the San Fernando Valley was in need of a house-sitter and baby-sitter. They were Catholics and had ties with a priest we knew back in New Jersey. When they told him of their problem, he immediately suggested they get in touch with us. We, upon hearing of an opportunity to get away from our crowded motel room, loaded up the kids and moved to the San Fernando Valley.

Here was another interesting situation. We had just relocated to a strange city and taken charge of six children (and a dog) plus our own three children in someone else's house! Thank heaven for Leona. She was the one who had the most difficult task. I went to work every day, but she was left behind to manage the situation. To her credit, she did a remarkable job. After three weeks, the people came home from their trip and found everyone healthy and happy (including the dog).

But for us, there were a few unresolved problems. Our house was still not completed and we had no desire to return to the motel. We decided to seek the help of the real estate people who had sold us the house. They suggested we might be able to camp out in the model house in the tract at night, then vacate the premises each morning. It was a strange arrangement, but we jumped at it.

Shelly and Monsignor Michael O'Connor

XIV.

Finally, our house was completed and we slowly tried to settle into the mellow California life style. Needless to say, though, our motors were still running at a New York pace. We were rolling along at 78 rpm while the natives were at 33-1/3.

Leona and I were beginning to feel the psychological strain of the move. I remember speaking with her one morning when all of a sudden she just burst into tears. "We'll never have any friends," she said. Indeed I was probably thinking along similar lines, but how very wrong we both were. The Lord lead us to California for a reason. There was a purpose, as we would soon find out, and, yes, we would have many, many friends.

The church we chose was St. Mel in Woodland Hills. It was a large parish with a wonderful man as its pastor, Monsignor Michael J. O'Connor. The name reveals his Irish descent and he surely had the Irish sense of humor to prove it. Our initial meeting took place during that first summer. I was following the Lord's dictates and looking for an outlet for my newly found musical expertise. To my knowledge, St. Mel's didn't have a choir. So I applied for the job. With music in hand and much trepidation in my heart, I met with the Monsignor and asked if I might be of some help in forming an adult choir. I remember him saying that he had looked into my background and thought I might be suitable. I think his exact words were, "I've had you *investigated* and you will do just fine." In the years that followed, my relationship with Monsignor O'Connor became one of great satisfaction. Our minds were as one. We both felt we were doing the Lord's work. Monsignor O'Connor was open to everything I was doing and was very supportive.

An ad was placed in the church bulletin announcing our first choir rehearsal. In response, 100 people showed up! Monsignor made his introductions and then turned the podium over to me. I realized that it was of the utmost importance for me to create the correct impression with this group. If we were to work together successfully we would have to start with a firm foundation: strong belief in God and a strong desire to serve the people of God. The lessons I had learned in New Jersey now served me in good stead. The choir and I got along just fine. The reality of what we were doing really set in when the choir began to sing. I was now dealing with 100 people. Even though they were for the most part amateurs, the sound they generated by their voices was incredible. When we sang our first Mass, the walls of the church resounded with their voices and the congregation expressed their appreciation with thunderous applause. The choir members smiled and so did I. We all knew we were on the right track.

Friendships blossomed as they had in New Jersey, and the Cohens now became part of the California scene. My creative juices were really flowing now, and I found myself totally immersed in writing religious music. My job was secure with *The Tonight Show,* so financially I had no worries. All my musical energies were now focused on making St. Mel's Adult Choir the best it could possibly be.

Composing music for the church posed some very unusual problems though. The main one being how to present my kind of music without offending the people who were used to a more traditional approach and at the same time appealing to the younger members of the parish. My philosophy about the music we have in our church today is this. Our young people are very much influenced by the society and the times in which we live. They are for the most part exposed to music with a beat. It's all around them—on the radio, in commercials on television. It's the kind of music they like. But, in most cases, when they enter a church they find themselves going back in time. They're entering a museum. The music they hear sounds foreign to them. It's beautiful, it's traditional, but it often fails to make a connection with the world outside the church.

I came up with the idea of trying to blend the old music and the new in such a way that everyone would be able to find something familiar in the music being sung at Mass. There might be an Ave Maria or Panis Angelicus for the more traditional ears and compositions with a strong beat for the younger people. Of course, it's impossible to satisfy everyone, and on one occasion I found myself being berated by a parishioner for using drums and guitars in church. I remember listening respectfully, then referring him to one of my favorite scripture readings, Psalm 150, where the psalmist tells the people to "praise the Lord with clanging bells and crashing cymbals."

But mostly we succeeded at St. Mel's and brought many new musical sounds to the church. On Christmas and Easter, I would augment our small instrumental group to include trumpets and strings. The sounds were glorious and the people responded enthusiastically. Sometimes the emotion was visible in the form of tears or expressed with such elation that you could almost feel the love in the air.

The choir raised money for the church through concerts, bake sales and the like. In addition, we paid for our own printed music and hired our own musicians. It was a very unusual situation, but the choir felt we could do it, and we did.

Along the way, I was fortunate enough to produce two Christmas specials for NBC. The shows featured members of The Tonight Show Orchestra and the St. Mel's Choir, of course. In addition, we made several recordings, one of which received a Grammy nomination. But the most important work we were doing was in our parish community. That was what it was all about: service to God and to His people.

XV.

It's not very often a person is given an opportunity to express his artistic gifts in a special way. I was fortunate enough to have been given that opportunity. I was asked by Father Gerard Weber to write music for an audio tape of the Rosary that ACTA Publications in Chicago wanted to produce.

I had a vague notion as to what the Rosary is about, but the specifics had eluded me. Enter Leona. She became my guide. She knew the Rosary well and explained its 15 mysteries and demonstrated the use of the prayer beads. She told me how important it was for the person praying this devotion to focus on each mystery and how it made the repetition of the prayers more meaningful.

I plunged ahead with my co-writer, Joe Mazza, and wrote the appropriate words and background music, keeping in mind all Leona had told me. To date, ACTA has sold about 100,000 audio cassettes and video tapes of the Rosary, both in the United States and overseas. For me, the project was a labor of love. And perhaps that is the real reason for it's success.

But unanswered questions still persisted. There was more for me to learn, more to understand about my newly found religion. True Jordan was back in New Jersey, so for all intents and purposes, Leona and I were on our own. Or so we thought. Once again the good Lord brought someone special into our lives.

We were fortunate enough to meet a Franciscan priest, Father Tony Scannell, who volunteered to help us continue our journey of discovery. With his guidance, we organized a discussion group. Once a month it met, and we immediately felt the Holy Spirit working again in our lives. The group stayed together for almost eight years and we all shared our lives with one another. We grew in knowledge and in the Spirit. It was a wonderful time for everyone, but unfortunately it ended when two of our members died.

The discussion group had been so very rewarding for Leona and me that we felt it shouldn't end there. But how could we fill this void in our lives? What could we do on our own? We believed we didn't have the knowledge necessary to go forward. We prayed on it, and we then found the answer to our prayers.

We decided to organize another discussion group, but this time it would be for people between the ages of 25 and 30 (both married and single). Leona and I would be the only "old fogies." There wasn't anything quite like that in our church.

We recruited about 15 or so people from the choir and presented them with the idea. They thought it would be fun. And so we began. We organized the group along lines similar to our previous discussion group and it worked. We've been together now for almost nine glorious years of loving and sharing. Lifetime friendships have blossomed, marriages have taken place, babies have been born. But most of all, we've seen the Holy Spirit working in each of us. I cannot fully describe the bonds created by our many shared experiences. Perhaps the best way would be to say: Jesus came among us and said, "Love one another." And we listened, and we were not disappointed.

Shelly rehearsing St. Mel's choir

XVI.

Our choir "family" was a dedicated group of people whose belief in Christ was very apparent. It was visible in our singing and in the way we treated one another. If there was an illness or death in the group, all would rally 'round and help. We prayed together and cried together. Christ's message of love was in everything we were doing.

But sometimes life doesn't always deal us a perfect hand. Sometimes there's trouble, and it's how you face that trouble that tells you and those around you where you stand with the Lord. Sometimes you're tested in such a way that your faith is shaken. I was put to that test . . . . and I was found wanting.

It happened a few years ago when a new pastor came to St. Mel's Church. I had known him several years earlier as one of Monsignor O'Connor's assistants and was looking forward to working with him. But that was not to be. His feelings about the liturgy and especially about the music for the Mass were quite different from mine. There seemed to be a wide and insurmountable chasm of understanding between us.

Finally the day came when I felt, after 20 years of service to St. Mel's Church, that I was no longer needed. I was being forced to leave. Leona and I discussed the situation at great length and decided that my health and happiness was much more important than supervising the music at St. Mel's. I went to the pastor and resigned my position. Then I spoke with the choir, giving them as much insight into my decision as I could. They were crestfallen and could hardly believe their ears.

We were all saddened by my decision and felt the coming void in our lives. We knew this loss was more than just the singing. St. Mel's was our home. Our children and grandchildren had been baptized there. Our choir families had made their first communion, been confirmed and been married at St. Mel's. I remember many of the choir members returning home with us that evening and bringing wine and cake, so we might share a few simple things for a little while longer. It was very much like a wake. People were sobbing but trying to keep their spirits up together. There was a genuine outpouring of love, and Leona and I felt it. But there didn't seem to be any alternative to the decision. I had to leave.

XVIII.

The pain I endured was one thing. But the anger building up within me was another. Why had God allowed this to happen? How could I ever go back into a Church where I no longer trusted the priests? That anger was blinding me.

About one week after my resignation, the pastor contacted the choir members and set up a meeting where he might present his perspective of the situation. I was not present, but the sense of the get-together, as I later found out, revolved around one point. Would the pastor agree to meet with Shelly once again and try to resolve their differences? Despite impassioned speeches from choir members, the pastor elected not to meet with me. It was over, finished.

Soon after that meeting, we had a goodbye party at our home. At the end of the party we sang together for the last time. We sang with tears in our eyes and much sadness in our hearts. It was then God's hand once again reached out and touched us. Several of the members suggested we should stay together even though we would not be affiliated with a church. We could still do good works in the community but, more importantly, we would still be together as a family. I wasn't sure it could work but I was willing to try.

We selected a committee to look into the matter and they came up with a viable plan. Yes, we would try to stay together. We would put on concerts for needy causes within our community, with all monies going to the sponsoring organizations. One of our members donated a rehearsal hall. We were off and running again. It has been almost five years since "The New Horizon Singers" had their debut, and from all indications, it looks like we'll be around for a long time to come.

But what about me? Where is Shelly Cohen, the convert to Catholicism, the new Christian? Up until the writing of this manuscript, I felt defeated, as if I had made one big mistake. But today, though my feelings about the Church are somewhat tarnished, all is not lost.

The New Horizon singers have received many invitations to sing at various churches in the area and even for the Cardinal. But more importantly, we have kept our original choir resolve to serve God, love one another and share our gifts with the people. The future for me and my family is secure. We have moved to another community and are once again getting involved in church activities.

"Yes, Suzie, I had to convert to Catholicism, because I do believe in Jesus." I never had the opportunity to actually say those words to her, but I certainly have thought them. God's plans for me, though not apparent in the beginning, seem a bit clearer now. He keeps on saying, "Take up your cross and follow me."

But He never said it would be easy.

A home Mass at the Cohen's

The New Horizon Singers in Concert

ACKNOWLEDGMENTS

When Greg Pierce of ACTA Publications asked me to tell my conversion story at dinner one evening, I said, "Sure, do you have half an hour?"

I've told my story many times and the telling has always given me a mild high. Sometimes the narrative was lengthy and at other times more succinct. But it has always intrigued the listeners.

After hearing my tale, Greg asked if I would take the time and put my story on paper. My immediate reaction was negative. I am primarily a music writer, and although I have written some poetry and a bit of prose I did not feel qualified to undertake this kind of project.

My wife, Leona, with considerable prodding, talked me into at least trying. For her perseverance and love, I am truly grateful. For in the writing I have rediscovered some of my earlier feelings about God.

Father Gerard Weber, who was present at that dinner with Greg, agreed to become my editor and ultimately my spiritual advisor. His keen literary expertise and encouragement added greatly to my text. For his contribution, I am forever in his debt.

There is one other person who I would like to acknowledge. Her name is Linda Vanek. She is a close personal friend, a super typist and a terrific syntax person. She has a fine alto voice and sings with The New Horizon Singers.

Without these people this book could not have been written. But the real inspiration came from the Holy Spirit, whose presence I felt from the moment I put down my first words. The message I received was this:

"Be open to God's gifts,

for they are given with love."

Devotional Tapes by Sheldon Cohen

The Rosary. The bestselling recording of all fifteen mysteries of the Rosary, with original meditations and music. Seventy minute audio cassette, $9.95; compact disc, $14.95; video, $19.95. Also available in Spanish on audio cassette, $9.95.

O Holy Child: Christmas Carols for Contemporary Christians. A glorious production of traditional and contemporary Christmas carols with full orchestra and choir, including two new original Christmas songs composed by Sheldon Cohen: *O Holy Child* and *The Christmas Rose*. Forty minute audio cassette, $9.95; compact disc, $14.95.

The Stations of the Cross. The traditional Way of the Cross, with each of the fourteen stations accompanied by prayer meditations and original music. Forty-five minute audio cassette, $8.95; video, featuring The Grotto in Portland, Oregon, $19.95.

Dona Nobis Pacem. Eleven hymns performed by The New Horizon Singers, featuring soprano Laurie de Santis, including Bizet's *Agnus Dei*, Frank's *Panis Angelicus*, and the Shubert and Bach-Gounod versions of the *Ave Maria*. Forty minute audio cassette, $8.95.

The Litanies with Music. Five of the most popular litanies with original music, including the litanies of the Saints, Holy Name, Sacred Heart, Our Lady of Loreto and St. Joseph. Thirty minute audio cassette, $8.95.

Novenas with Music. Four novenas with meditations and text by Rev. Lawrence Lovasik, including novenas to Our Lady of Perpetual Help, the Sacred Heart of Jesus, St. Jude and the Divine Infant Jesus. Thirty minute audio cassette, $8.95.

And Jesus Said. Readings of some of the best known sayings of Jesus, followed by original songs and musical reflections. Thirty minute audio cassette, $8.95.

Meditations with Music. Twelve 2-3 minute musical meditations on some of the most magnificent passages from the Psalms and other Scripture. Thirty minute audio cassette, $8.95.

Available through Christian bookstores or call 800 397 2282